Celebrations and Other Poems

David J. Murray

iUniverse, Inc.
New York Bloomington

Celebrations and Other Poems

Copyright © 2009 by David J. Murray

All rights reserved. No part of this book may be used or reproduced by any means, graphic, electronic, or mechanical, including photocopying, recording, taping or by any information storage retrieval system without the written permission of the publisher except in the case of brief quotations embodied in critical articles and reviews.

The views expressed in this work are solely those of the author and do not necessarily reflect the views of the publisher, and the publisher hereby disclaims any responsibility for them.

iUniverse books may be ordered through booksellers or by contacting:

iUniverse
1663 Liberty Drive
Bloomington, IN 47403
www.iuniverse.com
1-800-Authors (1-800-288-4677)

Because of the dynamic nature of the Internet, any Web addresses or links contained in this book may have changed since publication and may no longer be valid.

ISBN: 978-1-4401-7707-1 (sc)
ISBN: 978-1-4401-7705-7 (dj)
ISBN: 978-1-4401-7706-4 (ebk)

Printed in the United States of America

iUniverse rev. date: 11/12/2009

CONTENTS

Introduction ix

TREPIDATIONS

Too Much to Lose 2
Safety 3
How Could I Leave …? 4
I Could Not Move 5
Unsullied? 6
Both of You 7
Visions 8
Where the Wind Blows 9
A Sudden Blush 10
Never Will Mornings Rise 11
Winter Days 12
The Heat Grew Hot 13
Rains and Mists 14
I Cannot Move 15
Temptation 16
Self-Delusion 17
Premonition 18
Here We Go Again 19
Cliff-Cleft 20
Idling in Neutral 21
Brooding 22
In the Cool Night Air 23
Not the Same 24
A Stable Fifty 25
And Now the Quiet 26
Why Here? 27
Clarity 28
Knowledge 29
Daring 30
New Life 31
All I Need Do 32
The Only Peace 33

In the Blackest Night I Woke 34
Internal Warfare 35
A Muddy Grey 36
Fighting. 37
Truth or Consequences 38
Don't Talk 39
Untitled. 40
Resultants 41
As the Sunset Falls. 42
Christmas, 1986 #1. 43
Christmas, 1986 #2. 44

CELEBRATIONS

Mother's Day, May 9, 1992. 46
Birthday, June 8, 1992 47
Wedding Anniversary, July 5, 1995 48
St. Valentine's Day, February 14, 1996 49
Mother's Day, May 11, 1996. 50
Birthday, June 8, 1996 51
Wedding Anniversary, July 5, 1996 52
St. Valentine's Day, 1997. 53
Birthday, June 8, 1997 54
Mother's Day, May 10, 1998. 55
Wedding Anniversary, July 5, 1998 56
Christmas, 1998 57
St. Valentine's Day, 1999. 58
Mother's Day, May 9, 1999. 59
Birthday, June 8, 1999 60
Wedding Anniversary, July 5, 1999 61
(When we met). 61
St. Valentine's Day, 2000. 62
Birthday, June 8, 2000 63
Wedding Anniversary, July 5, 2000 64
Christmas, 2000 65
St. Valentine's Day, 2001 66
Mother's Day, May 13, 2001 67
Birthday, June 8, 2001 68

Wedding Anniversary, July 5, 2001 69

Christmas, 2001 70

St. Valentine's Day, 2002 71

Mother's Day, May 12, 2002 72

Easter, 2002 73

Birthday, June 8, 2002 74

Wedding Anniversary, July 5, 2002 75

"Normal Retirement Date," August 31, 2002 76

Christmas, 2002 77

St. Valentine's Day, 2003 78

Mother's Day, May 11, 2003 79

Birthday, June 8, 2003 80

Wedding Anniversary, July 5, 2003 81

Christmas, 2003 82

New Year, January 1, 2004 83

St. Valentine's Day, 2004 84

Mother's Day, May 9, 2004 85

Sixtieth Birthday, June 8, 2004 86

Wedding Anniversary, July 5, 2004 87

Christmas, 2004 88

St. Valentine's Day, 2005 89

Easter, 2005 90

Mother's Day, May 8, 2005 91

Birthday, June 8, 2005 92

Wedding Anniversary, July 5, 2005 93

Christmas, 2005 94

St. Valentine's Day, 2006 95

Mother's Day, May 14, 2006 96

Birthday, June 8, 2006 97

Wedding Anniversary, July 5, 2006 98

Christmas, 2006 99

New Years Eve, December 31, 2006 100

St. Valentine's Day, 2007 101

Easter, April 5, 2007 102

Mother's Day, May 13, 2007 103

Birthday, June 8, 2007 104

Thirty-Fifth Wedding Anniversary, July 5, 2007 105

Christmas, 2007 106
St. Valentine's Day, 2008 107
Easter, March 23, 2008 108
Mother's Day, May 11, 2008 109
Birthday, June 8, 2008 110
Wedding Anniversary, July 5, 2008 111
Thanksgiving, 2008 112
Christmas, 2008 113
Death Day Bedroom #1, Intensive Care Unit, Kingston General
Hospital February 5, 2009 114
Funeral Day James Reid Memorial Chapel, Kingston, Ontario
February 10, 2009 115
Interment Day Cataraqui Cemetery, Kingston February 12, 2009 116
Headstone Dedication Day, June 6, 2009 117

INTRODUCTION

This volume is the fourth in a series of volumes of assembled poems, some written many years ago, others written very recently. *Confusion Matrix and Other Poems* (2007) was a rather dark admixture of optimism and pessimism about the human world in general. *Surface Tension and Other Poems* (2008) was mainly taken up by an account of a Dante-like journey from the vicissitudes of a relationship with a woman with whom I encountered unexpected contentions concerning what was expected from that relationship, through a purgatorial state where brain and emotion seemed always to be feuding, to a final state, symbolized by "air and sky," characterized by a peace and lack of ambiguity engendered by my meeting with somebody whose ideals were close to mine. *War-Wise and Other Poems* (2009) contained a collection of poems (written, by request, in 2008) describing how my eight-year-old mind was affected by the events of World War II, including the Holocaust; I was a schoolchild in England from 1939 to 1945. That third volume also included a set of 100 poems that were basically technical exercises in versification, with the underlying theme being the splendours and miseries of romance.

This fourth volume is also solidly based on reality. In 1972, I married the girl who had inspired the "air and sky" section of *Surface Tension and other Poems*. Our marriage lasted thirty-six years before she was struck down by a succession of illnesses, including a disorder that seriously affected her ability to walk. The lyrical verses addressed to her in *Surface Tension* had all been written between 1970, the year in which we first met, in Montreal, and 1972, the year in which we were married there. We became parents four years later. The next twenty years were spent in the usual flurry of work pressures and family demands, but, in 1992, I felt constrained to write a poem to her on the occasion of Mother's Day that year; and, with increasing frequency, from 1992 until the end of 2008, I gave her a new poem, handwritten on a card appropriate to the occasion, on birthdays and other celebratory days each year.

After she died on February 5, 2009, I retrieved all those cards (not having re-read any of them since I wrote them) with a view to ascertaining whether I would wish to publish the poem each card contained. It is easy to criticize those poems for being "over the top" in sentimentality and in rhetoric; I was afraid I would not find them good enough to put into print. Following some editorial advice, I decided to publish nearly all of them. The last poem she herself read was from Christmas 2008, but I added four poems afterwards to complete the collection of seventy-eight poems, here entitled *Celebrations*.

Our marriage, however, like most, had its ups and downs. Among those downs was a tendency on my part, throughout my marriage, to be attracted

David J. Murray

to other women. In fact, nothing of note ever happened in any of these half-baked, purely mental, liaisons. Nevertheless, it intrigued me that, despite my devotion to my wife, I was not only capable of, but actually relished, the adventure of being involved, even at only an imaginary level, with more than one woman. It has been said that men are polygamous, women are monogamous; I suspect that this aphorism might be statistically valid, but it takes too lightly both women's polyamorous proclivities and men's desire for stability and family. Still, the old definition of marriage as a "tender trap" certainly resonates with married men who feel they are missing out, not necessarily on sexual variety, but on the thrill of the chase.

In retrospect, now that I am single again, I feel guilty about those all-too-many fantasies about other women, and I will almost certainly feel ambiguous, for the rest of my life, about the fact that some of those other women actually inspired me to write poems about them. But the major motivation that underlay my decision to publish a collection of some of these poems to other women, was neither concupiscence nor conceit. It was fear. When I was writing poems about those persons, I knew, deep inside myself, that if I were to act upon my promptings to infidelity, there would be disastrous financial and emotional consequences for everybody concerned. So nothing happened, except that these fears intrude consistently into what ought to have been straightforward complimentary verses. The title of this collection of forty-three poems, *Trepidations,* was determined by the pervasive anxiety it represents.

I am most grateful to Sylvia Haines, Rachel Breau and Christine Hains for helping me transfer the poems of *Celebrations* from my handwritten cards, and the poems of *Trepidations* from old-fashioned typescript, into electronic format. I am also grateful to the editorial and design teams at iUniverse, whose high standards enticed me, after *Confusion Matrix and Other Poems* had appeared, to want to publish as much of my verse as I could with their company.

I should like to dedicate this volume to the medical students, nurses, and specialists at Kingston General Hospital for the care and expertise with which my wife was treated during her final hospitalization from January 12 to February 5, 2009. I also wish to dedicate this volume to our family doctor, Dr. Katherine Kilpatrick, and to the team of health professionals working at Health for Life alongside Dr. Kilpatrick, for the skill they devoted to both of us during the two years or so prior to Esther's leaving us.

TREPIDATIONS

TOO MUCH TO LOSE

I heard the family-babble of my home,
The scuffling of the dog, the practised sounds
That floated from the piano, the radio's crackle,
And I knew I had no power to overcome
Their quiet relentless grasp; I could not tackle
The breaking of the cable from its grounds.

But as I wafted, half in sleep and waking,
From the pure noise that says a family's well,
Thoughts of your quiet and peaceful image floated
From them to thoughts of you, and, all-forsaking,
I wandered to my other world, denoted
By a hanging-on to you I can't dispel;

But there's too much to fear, too much to lose,
If I were forced between the two to choose.

SAFETY

Home: when I see, in panoply unhaltered,
Books, cups and saucers, cat, and battered bowls,
And think that, for a fortuned face unaltered,
I could exchange a fortuned family's goals,

I turn and slide and stare athwart the door;
Outside, the snow falls silently on cars,
And winds enrustle through the valley floor,
And in the bitter dark there are no stars;

I turn and look aback at our possessions,
The chair, the rug, that cost so much, that stands
As a golden symbol of our paired obsessions
With a safety only madness understands;

I cannot let these go, so quietly end
My dreams of knowing you better than a friend.

HOW COULD I LEAVE ...?

Now is my life nor flame nor ice nor cold
But just a mild incompetence; but how,
In consciousness, could I reject the old
If breaking it would break the very now?

How could I leave what strong emotion held
Together for years, through dark and light and grey,
Follies foretold for aeons and dispelled,
Lightness of mutual thought that summed each day,

And long unencumbered quiet familiar growth
That banished other follies from my heart
To relegated might-have-been, while youth
Upheld my marriage from the very start?

Yet, in your beauty, you shall always be
Quiet quickener of my verse and thus of me.

I COULD NOT MOVE

Within the solemn cradle of my love
Rides a quiet child, the moment when we met;
Your eyes were filled with strength; I could not move,
But all my mind was filled with my own debt

Of obligation and of past affection;
No one can fight the net of shared pain,
No one can fight unrecognized perfection,
And no one wants to start to sigh again;

I could not move, but felt my heart asunder;
Trapped was I fast between two equal treasures;
And all I did was make a stupid blunder
That blocked me off from all your store of pleasures;

But still I am whole, and, though I would go under
Were you both lost, I still both riches plunder.

UNSULTED?

No wit, no bitter, kind, recalcitrant sage,
Can say what kind of future may have lain
Before our wide and one-time eyes' embrace,

Except that, if it augured for an age
A mutual sameness born of equal brain
And swift approximation in our face,

We would have stood unsullied by cold Time,
And held our hands in hankerings of hope
That what, in a single moment, seemed forever,

Would have outlasted the faint and thought-felt crime
Of smashing another's life; but there's no scope
For mutual good if evil comes to sever

The linkage-bonds that love links to what's right;
So we cast down our eyes in mutual fright.

BOTH OF YOU

I cannot tell what faint reverberant light
Shines, like a slight refulgent inner coal,
Within my stormy, and yet peaceful, soul
That sees you both as partners of night

Within the long late night-time of my life;
Into the night I could walk equally
With either of you, or, regretfully,
Take both of you to be my wedded wife—

Regretfully, because there is a part
Of me that grew in strong and true belief
That one romance, no matter if a brief,
Would satisfy the longing in my heart;

But now I know new longing far too strong
To lose, with strength, each one of you for long.

Visions

When, into sheerness, dawn's deep veil ascends,
And lifts the light of nature to the sky,
Exciting clouds to chorus till night ends,
And shadowed grassblades into verdant cry,

Dawn lifts, in sheerness, all the veiled cases
Of blocked fixation and recalcitrance
That fill my married mind; and on dawn races
Till, in its free unhaltered pursuance

Of fuse of thought and nature, deeper it burrows,
And resurrects quiet visions of quiet fields
That lie beneath the brown unhurried furrows
Of burning cloud that soon to sunlight yields;

These visions come, and each is like a day
In the long suffuse of dark when you're away.

WHERE THE WIND BLOWS

So now you know, O infinite worshipful One,
That I am more than twice your age; I sigh,
With many a groan, of pasts that have long gone;
And cannot now act Romeo with your eye.

And yet what happiness I feel, despite!
How can this be, that, with your lovely youth,
You do not dare to mar this quiet respite
From all my younger yearnings for your troth?

I woke this morning, plagued by inner peace
That played guitarlike on my sense of guilt;
How could I know today would mark release
From all that clouded up my soul like silt?

Now we are free, both you and I; we know
That, where the wind blows, there we both shall go.

A SUDDEN BLUSH

A sudden blush of half-caught comprehension
Fails in a subtle way to break the mask
That a long and lifetime marriage's pretension
Makes of a face that no one takes to task,

And so these looks go vagrant. Unrequited,
Morals fix firm the requisite mien and pose;
The happiness that would have been invited
By a mere looking flashes, fades, and goes;

And all the quiet and unrecalcitrant meetings
That would have followed from a tender glance
Are dissipated into noisy greetings
And false effusions in a social dance;

Hiding a love turns sober men to serious;
Love is relentlessly imperious.

NEVER WILL MORNINGS RISE

I see your face, but never will mornings rise
When the first sight, in light of the glowing morning sun,
Will be the lustrous sparkle of your eyes,
And the first new act an inner orison

Of thanks that you are with me; all of this
Is just a dream, and you will go your way
And I continue in my work, and miss
The meetings that we now have day to day.

But dark will be the emptiness I'll feel
When you are gone, and inner landscapes shake
To dreary gardens, where the weeds congeal
To clumps of rainy wetness, and the lake

No longer shines with lustre, and the trees
Grow black and brown with winter as they freeze.

WINTER DAYS

So a quiet longing, and a Christmas greeting,
You with a cold, and me with deadlines strict,
Set up a pipe dream, waste and derelict,
That haunts the weeks that wait before re-meeting.

Just like the evening, the winter days ahead
Sink in a desolate sameness from day to day;
Overhead, the clouds are ragged grey,
With snow that sinks, like slumber, on the dead;

And all that winter tells us we possess
Is moral knowledge we have done aright
In not advancing forward on desire—

But, in our deepest hearts, that inward fire
Still glows quiescent in this inward night,
And still with crescent heat could incandesce.

THE HEAT GREW HOT

A marriage cycle in a clutch of days—
That is the way the heat grew hot, then went,
As feelings grew from neutral grey to haze,
And then subsided, sad and somnolent;

And yet the end seems nowhere far or near:
I saw you as you sat with muffler drawn
To shield you from the cold, and felt a fear
My feelings were too strong to be withdrawn;

A quiet sense of something new, paternal,
Filled me as I saw you sitting there
With your look that seemed a female sempiternal,
As light reflected from your shining hair:

And I felt, with instinct born of new suffusion,
That all my straightness merely brought confusion.

RAINS AND MISTS

The golden rains of spring quench summer thirst
And ancient winter moods should be dispelled;
Yet sadness comes with rain, for, roles reversed,
This food for flowers brings doubt unparalleled:

Where is the hope that summer will bring light,
When summer's only source is lost in mists?
How dare I hope to greet you in the night
With my age, and wedded state, antagonists?

How dare I hope one day to tightly hold you
In a nonpaternal grip that speaks my heart,
When youth's responsibilities enfold you,
And you, as well, do not know how to start?

The bitter rains of springtime speak of sin;
I hardly dare to know how to begin.

I CANNOT MOVE

And is that, then, a treachery to state
That, though I think of you as part of me,
I cannot move to hold and integrate
That thought? All I can do is silently

Re-contemplate your essence and write, quiet,
That, though you bring this essence to my world,
I cannot stretch my hand out to apply it,
Even to touch your hair where it lies curled;

For, if I dared to interrupt this mood,
And, in a stark and wholly physical way,
Brought you within my sphere, I would delude
Myself that I could simply throw away

All that my wife has offered me for years;
No, all I can do is write to ease my fears.

TEMPTATION

If all of this is infinite delusion,
Why is delusion easier than fact?
There is no greater source of heart's confusion
Than marriage vow betrayed in faithless act;

But when I see you sitting there, alone,
I have no thought of solemn marriage bed,
But only of the golden upright throne
On which I'd queen you, were you mine instead;

And when I stand beside you, and my hand
Is tempted to reach out to touch your hair,
I wonder if my wife would understand
How I desire you both and do not care

One to renounce, or the other to abjure …
Perhaps true love is only for the pure.

SELF-DELUSION

And then there are the hardened lines of years
That stand, like long enticing strands of warm
That guarantee quiet thoughts, and stifle fears,
And speak of warrior fights against real harm;

One cannot take the mettle of a life
And, in one fast discomfited sweep, embrace
A new, and torrid, start with a new wife,
As if the first had somehow brought disgrace,

When this were lie and lie and lie and lie;
It is something more, a fine and lively need
That cannot bear for part of me to die
In order that my wife need never bleed,

Yet, at the same time, cannot find the "no"
That would persuade the other girl to go.

PREMONITION

I ask, can worlds revolve and spheres collapse
In all this universe of soul that spins
On, quite unencumbered by relapse
To pastnesses of sighs where no one wins?

The only collapse can be of will and brain;
To stop this onward stream so strong and soft,
My present marriage, that never seems to wane
And holds me in its current borne aloft—

To stop this flow, would be a suicide;
And yet to renounce that serious part of me
That reaches out to hold you, would divide
My mind in two: the now, and what would be

A future filled with doubt if I forewent
The chance to hold you if you gave consent.

HERE WE GO AGAIN

If I were cool and quite disinterested,
Your letter, quite impersonal, could be delayed;
But there is something driving in my head
That makes me lose the part of me that's staid:

It registers a curse on seeing the mail
Dealing with money, and not a line from you,
And if I feel that, once again, I'll fail
To win a love because I gave no due

To longing longings in my married mind,
And life becomes once more a thing of rain,
Then I'll admit that I am stupid-blind,
And once again flirtation ends in pain;

But all the time these poems speak the truth:
I love your eyes and happy heart and youth.

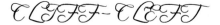
CLIFF-CLEFT

I had a dream, but dare not write of dreams;
The symbols were untraced, the riddles solved,
And loss is what the dream's deep meaning seems,
And I'm prepared to see my dreams dissolved.

So you are lost, a hammer over a cliff,
A smoke that crept on, up through a cleft, and went:
All these are symbols from my dream, but if
I followed up on dreams and what they meant,

How much of life would seem an empty dream—
How much of life would seem a sexless crawl,
A bumbling between meals, a silent scream,
An endless cloak of death about us all—

How much of life would seem to blow away
Like smoke, on a cliff top, on a windy day.

IDLING IN NEUTRAL

And, with a long fur-fretted sigh of tedium
That once again my poems are the medium

For sighs and tears and quiet recriminations
Of "what did I do wrong?"—the ministrations

Of you, my brain, to soothe my silly musings
Pour forth in wordy bricks scarce of my choosing;

I've been here before; I'm bored with artifice
That tries to prop up feelings like an edifice,

Saying "I will transform to utter beauty"
All the relinquishings of lovers' duty

Because of marriage and morals; but the truth is,
I did not fly to hie to where your youth is;

And, all the time my courage idles neuter,
I run the risk you're lost to a brave new suitor.

BROODING

When all seems dull and gloom and far away,
And the far trumpets scintillate with doom
Like the distant cries of gods of Hell who loom
High, low in the thunderclouds that play

On the horizon, and yet are only dreamed—
When all this seems like a play upon a stage,
And reality is a man of stable age
In a stable house, where turmoil only seemed

To play a part, is simply brooding wild—
When all the world that aches when love is lorn
Is somebody else's, not his, then is he torn
Not between mistress and family, trophy and child,

But only between two clashing greeds within:
Polygamy knocks, but cannot be let in.

IN THE COOL NIGHT AIR

And so the days spin on and on
With doggerel—"wondering where you've gone"—

Rhymes that strain to seem unforced,
And runes and rhythms undivorced

From solemn meaning and import;
But all this verse seems empty sport

When, in the dark of late-at-night,
I think about you, trying to fight

My guilt, while, in the cool night air,
My wife sleeps deeply, unaware

I've kept a silence on the fact
I think of you in every act,

Yet dare not phone you for the fear
I speak my feelings straight and clear.

NOT THE SAME

The wind was arch and cold and chill and sere;
The rain hung in the turgid air and swept
Each gust with wet, and brought a hidden fear
Of silent sadness and of tears unwept;

On days like this, I think it was a year
Ago, I wrote of emptiness that crept
To tangle in my work and seemed to shear
Into a cloud that made my verse inept;

And a year has gone, and now I still appear
A quiet and upright person who has kept
His life untangled, who can quietly steer
Novices on fertile roads he once had stepped.

But he is not the same; a major sun
Has shone upon a road he dared not run.

A STABLE FIFTY

A stable fifty, but somehow trapped in tardiness,
I find a new love for the young and the fit and the spry;
Each girl on the street sizzles with attractiveness
And sometimes I catch a come-on in her eye;

But I forget your age, your youth, your youngness;
I forget your life lies straight ahead and new;
I forget that you'd shrink from shackling your harness
To one who's twice as old, and tired, as you;

All I see is your hair in its prime and its glossiness;
The wonderful blue, that sparkles in your look,
Seems to frizzle my high and cognitive broodiness
Into a mellow murmur like a brook;

And all I can see is the possible golden fruition
If I were unmarried and followed pure intuition.

AND NOW THE QUIET

And now the quiet falls down in peace serene.
The rapt inordinate meadows of my hopes
Seem drained of their streams, but still remain in green,
While verdant apples grow upon green slopes;

And storms that ought, in times I've cried aloud,
To have hung, in dark foreboding, on the hills,
Seem to be quiet, just wistful trails of cloud,
While the sun the verdant valley quietly fills;

And, through this landscape, as I walk awake,
The dreamier side of marriage seems to stalk;
The planning of this and that, the give and take,
The simple chats that make a family's talk;

The storm you caused is quietly dying away
Like winter clouds upon an April day.

WHY HERE?

I cannot say I'm sad: she should not know
That in the distance, on the phone, exists
A somebody, me, whose moods of high and low
Depend on if she phones or she desists;

I cannot say I'm sad: I'm too mature;
I should, in mood of high and super reason,
Work on my work, and smile at being secure,
And never think to hurt my wife with treason;

I cannot say I'm sad: I'm happy too—
I'm happy at the warmth that fills our hearth,
At the joy of family fare the whole year through,
At the knowing that folks like me fulfill the earth;

Then why are these poems here? What is their aim?
They are too real to simply be a game.

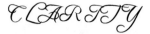
CLARITY

And, while the errant winds betray the sky,
The arc all blue, the winds all cold and dry,
The leaves that blow betray the inner fear
That all my life must now be dry and sere;

I cannot follow through when instinct calls.
I'm hemmed within a marriage's pure walls:
I cannot shout for fear that people stare,
Nor can I weep, for tears are just not there;

I must not go mad, with wild and follied thought,
Making a giant, with frantic frenzies fraught;
Nor must I stop and claim desuetude
Where obsolescence would oust gratitude;

So I go on, pretending what I am
Is what I am, and covering the sham.

And yet the sham is false; for I have written
That, in the follied hours that I've been smitten
With somebody not my wife, conciliation
Is found in dreams or some such sublimation—

No! What stands clear is that I cannot leave,
Abandon, desert, forsake those I believe
To truly offer what all men most need,
Comfort of bed and table, lack of greed,

No endless plaint to talk and entertain,
No hid contempt when failures come to strain
The fine white sheet of life's advancing,
And shreds of age reduce a man's enhancing—

No, all I have is what I most must keep …
But in my poem-world I'm free to weep.

KNOWLEDGE

The sun shines warm on gold October leaves,
And the blue sky seems to shun all thought of rain;
But he, who once has lost a love, believes
That simple sunshine always forecasts pain;

And, as the students walk from class to class
Thinking of fun and drink, the wise professor
Sees the uncaring youth that soon will pass
Into a sadder maturity, made the lesser

By sad refinement of straightforward lust,
By foolish mixings of desire with thought,
By all the lost experience that must,
Once mind is mixed with love, remain untaught;

And only those who've known a love uncrossed
Can know the pain when such a love is lost.

DARING

Because I dare to think you think of me,
And have felt a subtle tremor in your grace
As you talk, because you know that I can see
Your nervousness, and wish to hide its face,

I dare to think that maybe you think more
Than I dare hope, with our work unwell, and my age,
And the distance, and my wife, and things that passed before,
But, I confess, I would not dare to gauge

More than a passing friendship from that hope,
More than "How are you?" "Quite well, thanks" "Indeed!"
And a flattening of what once seemed in scope
A large erotic Everest of need;

But, over and again, we pass, in life,
Potential conquests and potential strife.

NEW LIFE

The winter winds blow cold upon my soul;
Or so I thought before your letter blew
New life into a dozing mind that knew
Better than let drear worry take its toll;

And a silly strike sent all the mail askew,
Including all your words that simply wrote
Of work and this and that, a simple note
That hid whatever favours were my due;

But all my talk of how my fancies float
Wild when I have no anchor for my dreams,
And all my mooning verse about what seems
Too far-impossible to be real antidote

To poisoned hopes, now seem to be unreal.
Words can be weary wards of what we feel.

ALL I NEED DO

The pain is simple, if I have your absence;
All I need do is write "goodbye" and lo,
A fitful sunshine falls across the silence,
And sends a shaft of light across the snow;

I can see clear, not forced, if free of you;
I can give light, not dark, to those I love;
I can write simply how all three of you—
Wife, daughter, you—combine to prove

That they possess my mind, and I must never
Clouden my life by veering off to you;
And yet, if you were here, I could not sever
Myself so simply with a mere adieu;

My heart would pound, I'd be so short of breath
That saying "goodbye" would seem like sudden death.

THE ONLY PEACE

The only peace, the only rest from thought,
The only idling in an idolizing day,
Is after love, when humours down-distraught
Fight to revive the life that flowed away;

And in that peace, I thank the female giver
Who brought a stop to anxious tension's hold;
I thank her and I know I must deliver
Peace in return, my love in place of gold;

And I feel then, in the glow of resting quiet,
With subtle tingling in my veins and arms,
That chiding peace, as if I would deny it,
Would only bring me tears and outright harms;

Yet afterwards, as through the streets I hurry,
I sense your absent presence, and I worry.

IN THE BLACKEST NIGHT I WOKE

In the blackest night I woke; I felt,
When I thought I had you, inmost deepest fear
That I could quite unwittingly uprear
And crash me down upon you as you knelt;

I felt such fear from power that maybe I,
Endeavouring, had won your winning heart;
How could I not feel fear, when in your eye
I felt you felt we'd never been apart?

I felt you felt I felt perhaps too shallow;
You felt I felt you felt you were too shy;
And, in the waiting days when time was fallow,
Perhaps we'd both built castles in the sky.

But, when you said we could not meet the morrow,
My one outstanding feeling was of sorrow.

INTERNAL WARFARE

My books, here on the desk, are all of grief:
Men murdering wives and women setting fires,
And most of them inspired by the belief
That round about them everyone conspires

To plot and cheat and knave them of their wealth;
All darkness comes from fear, and, as I read,
My mind cannot dispel a sense of stealth
Denizened by the fear I really need

You, the young you, the lovely wonderful you;
I feel I am drone to parasite my soul
To her who gave me back what I was due—
My self, and thereby made me once more whole—

My gratitude now is warring with my sense;
Conflict and care are all my recompense.

A MUDDY GREY

The sky is grey and no lights play
On the dark and snowy ground;
Between the trees a boring breeze
Flaps the leaves around;

The snow is black where autos back
Exhausts upon its murk;
A muddy grey fills all the day
And everyone hates work;

The empty sky, like you and me,
Seems waiting for completion;
The endless wait seems to berate
Our caution to depletion;

But, since we met, who can forget
We've never let our thoughts out yet?

FIGHTING

Once more I fight deep morals and am lost;
As the days roll by, and I read deep books, I sigh;
As I take cool baths, or eat fast meals, I try
To feel less battered and less tempest-tossed;

In summer nights' dark silences I'm crossed
With fears; beside my sleeping wife I lie,
With my head driven by dreams that you and I
Are alone and free to linger without cost;

And, in a dream, I quietly hold your hand;
The trembling nerves of true encounter join
In a great retrenchment of impediments;

We are alone and free to touch and sense,
And in a golden glade come loin to loin,
—And then the dream is blown away like sand.

TRUTH OR CONSEQUENCES

Strange behaviour waltzes time and hour:
An hour's confusion, judged amiss as nerves,
Serves to entail old memories' going sour,
And a list of just what faithlessness deserves;

This list is slightly tinged with emptiness,
That what one had within one's grasp was lost,
Not the result of anything said, or less
Of natural fervour, just a counted cost—

But what a cost: the bitter child, the edge
Of penury, the guilt and relic weight
Of being an abandoner, a wedge
Jammed in the jaws of family estate,

Opening, dividing, forcing grief and tears
That never dry across the passing years.

DON'T TALK

A speech that crushed and swept all lust aside
—Or did it? For, after the end of the speech, and the long
Walk through the streets, with me all sad inside,
And you in silent union with the throng

We moved a-through, and brushed in emptiness,
I said goodbye, and touched your arm, and thence
All chaos fired within me and no less
Than a seizing of you eased my insolence;

And now, by some mad psychology, I lie
In on mornings, dreaming of your touch,
And sail in solemn ecstasy to a sky
Of thought and dreams as if I dared too much;

For now that the thought is out and now you know
How much I owe my wife, my dreamings flow.

UNTITLED

Something cracked, my mind collapsed, and my hand
Reached out, and held you, and, in willow wisps,
The clamour of my lips received your lips,
And I fell back, conquered, shamed, and stunned.

And, now, I cannot move, because no end
Seems to exist between air and invisible chains
That bind me to you. Springtime pours its rains
On radiant landscapes nothing can transcend;

My bond is fixed and fine, and stays unblended
With older incompletions and ambitions;
I cannot let you go, or make conditions,
Without a sense of loss, unless I ended

The matter on rational grounds, taking a knife
To sever off my soul, but keep my wife.

RESULTANTS

The souring of the sap because of marriage,
The bringing hard to heel because of love,
The bridled labour of an ode's miscarriage,
The stifling of an instinct from above:

All are resultants of monogamy;
There's nothing can be said to change its sway;
All art, all verse are part of its monopoly,
And everything one thinks one scares away.

All hope, all power, all greater masculine thoughts
Are chased into a muddle by being wed;
A mighty veil of sinfulness disports
Its folds across what's dreamed instead of said;

And yet I cannot flee the marriage haven;
The fear of all the hurt hath made me craven.

AS THE SUNSET FALLS

And how, as the stage grows darker, ends the scene?
The light comes down, lowers the light on the stage,
The oak trees burn with tarnish on their green,
And verdant youth gives way to grimmer age;

Light is like nature caught in capering;
The radiant noon stands poised in crescent flight
Over the vernal branches, blazing spring
With archetypal lineage of light;

Then sunset falls, and black enfolds the sky;
Age will encompass all that gleams and grows,
And mark with her wrinkled white the passer-by
Who stoops to stare at the bulging blood-red rose;

But you have caught, as the sunset falls, a light
That age will never darken with its night.

CHRISTMAS, 1986 #1

Her homemade bread, with East Ontario cheese,
I hymn as part accompaniment to rhyme
That maybe is ephemeral as the breeze,
Or maybe will survive the end of time;

Her cheesecake, and her rich and rare desserts,
That sit, quiet sating, on our dining table—
These I revere till poetry reverts
To prosy syllables that are not able

To fuse a follied romance to a verse.
And if you think no metre suits roast goose,
Or distrust lines that seem a mite perverse
Because they render music to a mousse,

Then you, dear reader, have not met a cook
Whose lunches are as lovely as her look.

CHRISTMAS, 1986 #2

I smell the stew a-simmering on the stove,
And note the calm alertness of the cat;
The TV snorts and ad waves soar above
The clatter of the dishes and the pat-

Pat-patter of the dog's feet as he goes
To smell the latest savour from the pot,
And children's laughter quite torrential grows
As lingerie is found among the lot

My wife threw out—it's been there many years—
The Christmas tree shines winking lights galore,
And there's a rattle, as the mailman steers
His way between the screen and the front door

To leave more Christmas cards; and all of this
Could just go phut! in an adulterous kiss.

CELEBRATIONS

MOTHER'S DAY, MAY 9, 1992

And now the waltzes finish like a charm,
Broadened and burdened, sonics filled with air,
With the trumpet's flowerlike flute a-filled with flair,
Filling the air with freedom from alarm.

But when the waltzes end and ends the ball,
And only echoes flicker and faint in the mind,
Their meaning stays: they sang of womankind;
They sang of you, who made our home their hall.

BIRTHDAY, JUNE 8, 1992

Plunged in your long lost midnight of deep sleep
Your figure lies a-one with blankets, sheets,
And the window-light cascades upon the heap
You form with them till you move, and sleep retreats.

And then you rise, clear in the sunlight's glow,
But tired, with a somewhat mumbling in your mind
Till clearer thought wakes up and bids it go
And you move to a world that no one thought you'd find:

A world that is sometimes hard on selfishness,
Domestic, sometimes humdrum, day to day;
But this world is stronger than one that does with less,
That makes of partnership a "better" way.

But the world you have will not so easily fade;
Beauty will pass, but homes are solid made.

WEDDING ANNIVERSARY, JULY 5, 1995

You are the sun that lightens up my ship
When, skimming through the borderlands of seas,
I sometimes feel I fail to keep my grip
Upon the flailing sails, or feel I freeze;
You are the sun that fills my sail with ease;
You are the sun who never fails to please.

ST. VALENTINE'S DAY, FEBRUARY 14, 1996

Whiter than snow grows the white light of morning
And sends its cold rays through the curtain's cold net,
But the red gold of sunrise is still not adorning
Your head with its hallowing influence yet;

You sleep, and I look, and I see how your head
Rests on, in a stillness that wraps itself round you;
You sleep in the light of the growing sun's red
But I think of the night of the day that I found you;

Days and dead nights have gone by since that meeting,
Sunsets and mornings have moved on and on,
But I feel, as I feel how my sleep is retreating,
That I cannot imagine your ever being gone.

MOTHER'S DAY, MAY 11, 1996

As days wear on, with cold that's out of hand,
And rainclouds sweep and weep across the land,
Darkness enhances the light you represent;

And even when the flowers and tulips glow
In sunlight's flood, your light will brighter grow
And shine more brightly than their firmament.

BIRTHDAY, JUNE 8, 1996

All I can think, as home I make my way,
Is: I have no need to brood or sigh or flirt;
I have what I want; you always crown my day

With giving that I never can repay;
Never do I want to see us hurt
By others who would pull our hearts away;

Because, though rains may rift the sky with grey
And spatter plantdom with a cloud of dirt,
The sun you represent must always stay.

WEDDING ANNIVERSARY, JULY 5, 1996

Now, with the night all around me, I stand and I ponder
What moment or mood caused my footsteps to wander to meet you;
Now, in this darkness, I stand and I silently wonder
What blackness would fall if I ever forgot how to greet you;

I praise the enchanted solidity of your endeavour
To hold in a constant unity all that we've won;
I'll never forget all the hope that you gave me forever;
And darkness can never engulf what was wrought by your sun.

ST. VALENTINE'S DAY, 1997

And what if time should turn its tail and turn
Your aging lines to younger styles, more isle
Of Paradise a-heave, and less consistency?
Intensity speaks and renders more to howls
Than to long whines and gazes into glass;
A single moment, purged of the cares of its time,
Enters the memories full, engaging thought,
Turning one's backward vista to a film,
Making the past eventful, colouring it
With moments scored with acmes of success;
Such was the moment when, decades ago,
You showed to me your quiet emotional reason,
And soothed to life my deadening soul; and still,
It is such when you move, here in the light of the night,
To bring me to life and batten down the dark;
I can still move myself, with you the strong
And ever-watchful guardian of our hopes.

BIRTHDAY, JUNE 8, 1997

Though, through this angry world, some others shout
That others merit what I offer thee,
And, redolent of battle, some cry out
Concerning what is "right" and "fit to be,"

"One with the other," "two with each equal," sounds
That batter the air with e's and i's and o's
Till even daffodils droop from vowelly wounds
And mists of guff distil upon the rose;

Still, in this storm, an old song can be heard,
Striding ahead untrammelled though the hail
Of verbs and nouns and their ilk, forms of word
That rain upon the heads of those who fail

To understand the words of yesterday;
Its words are old: "Our love is here to stay."

MOTHER'S DAY, MAY 10, 1998

The years wear on and, darkling, in the night,
Come to me magnitudes of all your youth;
I see you, as if yesterday, in white,
Smiling, nuanced with simple-speaking truth;

The years, like chiaroscuro clouds a-race,
Wane; where was mist (the now) is clear (the past);
Thou smilest, beacon of our trysting place,
New Gaia in a role the Muses cast;

And, what is turning me still all tip-a-top,
Is that the years have kept you un-poseur;
What drove me then, with power I could not stop,
Enclenches me still to what you are and were.

WEDDING ANNIVERSARY, JULY 5, 1998

I have to hide my inner foremost words
For they are too harsh, too withering, of the minds
That others, more blatant than are you in dress
And folded armouries of talkiness,
Show to me, with their wont of more show-off-ness.
You, like me, are quiet, pleased just to read,
Adventure with fugues or quilts, spend hours
Sojourned with yearning that we know will end
In less than hours, so close are we in wanting
Silences saved from death by angels' demi-chants
To a nature who has moulded you to be
Form and enchantment for my whole contentedness.

CHRISTMAS, 1998

I'd kept our enchanted hours, as they passed by,
Half-telescoped in time, so keen were thieves,
Like "tardiness," or "happenstance," to blurt
Their noisy babble into ours and try
To tear off minutes like bedraggled leaves
And let them float, flat downwards, to the dirt;

I'd folded those hours, like moments of gold leaf,
Into pilastered alphabets for books
No saints shall contemplate in desert caves
Or gaze upon in poignant disbelief
Or mark for silent study in dark nooks
Of dusty temples built on dusty graves;

Those alphabets were waiting for the time
When I would form and rank them for this rhyme.

ST. VALENTINE'S DAY, 1999

A silence falls that pulls us closer to;
The emptiness is filled, at once, by us;
No pathways now exist to distance you
From me, nor roads that we must blunder through
To some dark drop of cliff precipitous;

There's just a thing of nothing, nothing, here,
Not needing words to give it depth and place,
Quite happy to be empty, cavalier,
Happy that words will never make it clear,
Persisting in its nothingness of space,

Persisting in its nothingness of sound,
Persisting in its nothingness of light;
And when the storms and winter ice abound,
And violent rainbows grind the sun aground,
Our silence will be our bond and our delight.

MOTHER'S DAY, MAY 9, 1999

The weeks move on, but solidly
You stand, like silken air
Framed within a mental strength
That gives me cause for prayer;

Silent, like light you stand, light
That plays on springtime's green;
Silent, not seeking attention,
A vision but unseen;

Your presence holds me firmly—
My self hangs on your vine,
And when the wind blows wildly,
You hold my self to thine.

BIRTHDAY, JUNE 8, 1999

I strive to hymn the hollowed hideaway
That drives me in bliss from humdrum everyday
To the entrenchment of your smoothened arms;
Night is turned white, and Graecian are your charms;

There are quiet arbours where your body looms,
Like fleshly flowers, each offering fresh blooms
Of happiness, gaud, and the haunted interplay
Of sleeping and waking that keeps my fears at bay;

There are moist anchors here where our ships partake
Of the long baylike daylight that floods the wide lake
While night overhead fills the ocean with stars
Dropped like glittering pools from Venus and Mars;

But mostly these rapturings fall from the sleeper;
As fiction dies down, facts grow the deeper.

WEDDING ANNIVERSARY, JULY 5, 1999 (WHEN WE MET)

I saw you through a vitrous pane of glass,
Perception, you, and round you played
Sounds and freak music and with you were
Mild people, lookers, standers, no one thinkers;
But you stood out, quiescent, wild and waiting,
And I reached out, through the wondrous waiting throng,
Touched you in the dress of woolen white
I still, in old protracted age, dream of you in,
Touched you and saw, in your bright and waiting eye,
What I desired, unquestioning, from you,
And won from you and still have from you
And still want from you and will always want
From you till the days are done, in golden mist,
With high pilasters of outrageous dawns, and doves
Skying, and silence, and dew on the lawn waiting
For somehow this chorus to enden, but enden
It will not so long as we wanten, we wanten …

ST. VALENTINE'S DAY, 2000

Silence sometimes is golden and sometimes is not;
And yet you allow me to think, and are rarely a scold
When I come from outside and announce what it was I forgot
To remember, despite being phoned and reminded and told

What I ought to remember to do and ought not to forget;
Yet part of my mind is enfixed like a superstrong chain;
It anchors my mind to my soul: with this link, I can let
All torrents that flow through the cliffs and the clefts of my brain

Storm themselves dry till all turmoil is settled and still;
You are that part; the chain was enforged when I met you;
So long as I dream of your hold and our home and your skill
With the nurturing matters of life, I can never forget you.

BIRTHDAY, JUNE 8, 2000

And, were it not for palisades of light
Flailing and joining where the fencing fits,
Only eventful ambuscades of night,
Fantasies, would flood the scenic sets

Of all this mental wanderlust of mine
With summer-filling fullness, banishing
Betrayals of the follied flaunts of wine,
And scaring silly social sorts to vanishing;

But thou, with increasing glint of gold and joy,
Enhancest occasional moments soured with dark
With unresisting unimplorèd ploy
That fires upended stockade-stakes to spark,

Scattering splendid fire-flames flame-ahigh,
Uplighting night, unlighting flight, Ur-Gemini.

WEDDING ANNIVERSARY, JULY 5, 2000

And when, in recognizance, glistering starsheets
Scatter your praises from earthsongs to skies,
The descant of denigrants rises and half-meets
The panoply, starfilled, that over All lies

And sends down the descant, cascading, to places
That hollow this Arcady, blackness and lightness,
Interstices blank with reticulate spaces,
Quietness boasting your infinite rightness,

And downwards, more downwards, it falls, still episcopate,
Throwing out, jettisoned, embers remembered
Of glowing, half-echoing, Natures unreprobate,
Minds, Myths and Madnesses, humbled, dismembered.

CHRISTMAS, 2000

Incarcerated where they one time grew,
Awaiting my behest,
Burst they again as if anew,
Poems I thought at rest;

Quiet is the sky that oversees
The budding of the day;
Blue are the lupins by the trees,
Luring the bees away;

Incarcerated where it one time grew
Inwardly in my brain
Bursts my verse fresh as if anew:
Summer has come again.

ST. VALENTINE'S DAY, 2001

When the winter starts to warm and wane again,
And the brownness fades, and the green begins to grow,
I feel the warmth within your heart regain
The heat that gave that heart its overflow;

And, as you watch for spring, scanning the wind
That blows away the sand that strews the lane,
I feel your heart has grown and re-attained
The glow that had been dimmed by winter's rain.

MOTHER'S DAY, MAY 13, 2001

And where in my small dark world of thought
Are you to fit? You match, like a lock,
The key of my hopes; your body is wrought
Still to fill me, on seeing you nude, with shock—

There's nothing to say; I can only hide
In my office and offer you spluttering verse
Whose pallid unmatching of what is inside
Your exterior person makes mine seem perverse;

And so, as I grey, and my fingers and hands
Slowly contort to self-blasphemies, I
Repeat, like a criminal, all those demands
That I made, when we met, that you never deny;

And, knowing your liking of endings that please,
I'll pretend you're a statue of limitless flesh,
And, just like a kid, I'll go down on my knees,
And ask to be caught up again in your mesh.

BIRTHDAY, JUNE 8, 2001

Into my winter's whirlwinds played my fate,
But you rebuffed it, proving that no gate
Is ever closed to searchers for the truth
Although that questing may have scorched their youth.

The gate you opened, vassal-like from Thor,
But dressed a-womanly for love, not war,
Starkened at first the contrast with the black
Of my hopelessness, the light of hope far back;

But, as it opened wider every day,
The black grew fainter, yielding to a play
Of lights that flowed from the further skies of all,
Guiding the search for the greatest prize of all:

True art accomplished before the end,
Verses a-throng whose office is to mend
Adversities and to absorb those tears
That, unallayed, still attest those years.

WEDDING ANNIVERSARY, JULY 5, 2001

If discontent should make some summer sour,
And longing surges drain an evening hour
Of sapience and happiness, strewing blight
To blur the radiance of that summer night,

My knowledge of the certainty that you
Would illumine the darkness, gild anew
The gold already crystalled from your gaze
From all those earlier years and yesterdays,

And surface to erase the bilious power
That buffeted my veins to render me dour;
I would know that, with your archly female breath,
You'd chase away my being-in-love-with-death,

And would, instead, ensconce me in your bed
Where, powered and motived by your lovely head,
I would enfold, within re-aureate arms,
Its blackness and its firmly boldened charms.

CHRISTMAS, 2001

My brain, unburdening, has forgot
To fill thy flowing bowl with verse
Of a kind in which my happy lot
With thee has kept a straitened heart
With odes that coldnesses reverse;

For age's aches do now enhance
The voiding of my pent-up mind;
I dream of a violent morbid dance,
A mordant let's-be-we-like trance,
Where grinning kings look on, unkind,

Where angels are mockers, lovers cold,
And youngness smells of growing old;
But when the dream stops, and I thee hold,
I know my happiness outgleams gold.

ST. VALENTINE'S DAY, 2002

Although the sun, in a midwinter glare,
Brightens the snow till it glistens like spring,
The air is cold, and the sky is so cold
That nothing can bolden the sparrows to sing;

No ray of warmth is piercing the air;
The sun is a rounded and glittering thing,
An ironfire, caught in its circle of gold,
Awaiting, in vain, for the birds to take wing;

But heat's in the house, and the heat is yours;
Your warmth fills the household, your heartbeat is ours
And the warmth, that you warm up my words with, endures

On this page, in a fashion that quickly empowers
An effluence of feeling that quickly ensures
That each moment can melt into hours and hours.

MOTHER'S DAY, MAY 12, 2002

The bird-calls of the forest wake
Their answering mates; the chirruppings
That chatter, through the branches, break
The silences of hidden wings;

Emotions animate the wood;
Silent, in blue, the white clouds float;
Nestlings betoken motherhood;
Its burrow hides the pregnant stoat;

And I dare not stand, intrusively,
Within the wood, but, at its edge,
Lie me in grass, exclusively
To think of you, of the privilege

Of hearing, touching, holding, seeing
All that is nature in your being.

EASTER, 2002

Invariate, inviolate in life,
You smooth the steady concourse of my path
As I rebuff vicissitudes of strife,
And frighten off the impishness of math;

For, though emotions carve the smoothened spheres
That constitute men's souls as slow they age,
Those spheres are often dented by brute fears,
And bended into bullet-shapes by rage;

But you are always there, you are never far;
You smoothen out the roughnesses of time;
And any memory that once implied a scar,
You cause to burst, instead, into a rhyme.

BIRTHDAY, JUNE 8, 2002

Although a rain brings grey on grey,
A shower can start a summer's day.

Although a cloud can cloud the sky,
A mist can make the flowers grow high.

And, though a dream can mar my peace,
Awakening gives me fast release,

For there you lie, beside my side,
No dream, but real, my sleeping bride.

WEDDING ANNIVERSARY, JULY 5, 2002

Because you wanted what I had,
You felt the best in me begin,
And the best in me began to win,
And the less the world seemed wholly bad;

But no philosophy can spark
Life from a soul that is almost dead;
Only a light like yours can shed
A glow that can grow inside that dark;

Nor can pure physics start to say
Why nothing matters more than you
When, in a perfect snapshot view,
You brighten the light of a summer day;

And reasoning, taints, and cults will pass
Before their tauntings dare to mar
My memory of thee as star
In a world that had splintered as if 'twere glass.

"NORMAL RETIREMENT DATE," AUGUST 31, 2002

Full I have known thee for one span of life.
Three spans exist: the start; the middle part;
The end. The start endowed my mind and art.
The middle was marked by mouldering fits of strife
Made peaceful by the works of thee, my wife.

Grandeur springs greatest when a passion reigns;
So strong is thy strong hold on me that I
Can never hold, for more than days, the lie
That, in my mind, my own hold quietly wanes;
Nothing can be more wrong; my passion *gains*

Therefrom in strength; I cannot see thee stand,
Blackened in silhouette against a light,
Without a closer move to grip thee tight,
Squeezing till sadnesses drift away like sand,
Holding thee firm till all our years are spanned.

CHRISTMAS, 2002

A dark and lasting gloom can summer spread
When nonreciprocation of a love
Fetters all joy and halts all urge to move
As if all hope had faltered, slumped and fled;

A mind can be encaptured by this dusk;
It fogs the now and casts unending shades
Upon a future where Arcadian glades
Seem only shadows, hollows in a husk;

But, on my darkness, you enforced your light,
And showed, not only me, but kin and friends,
That joy and love are not impossible ends,
But can be superposed on mental night;

And, though that night engendered poetry,
Enfertilized by hopings all the more,
Yesterday, when I saw, just near the door,
Your curving silhouette approaching me,

I knew no kind of verse, however strong,
Encaptures me like the strength of your embrace,
And no ill health, that keeps me from your grace,
Can stop me from encapturing you in song.

ST. VALENTINE'S DAY, 2003

The waves roll on and the tides roll on
And the wind rolls over the roiling sea,
But a place of peace resides in me
And will stay in me when the waves have gone;

Thou art my heart, thou art my gold,
Thou art the sun that heats my land,
Thou art the radiant, thou the grand,
Thou art the morning I watch unfold,

Spreading its rays across the lawn,
Whispering wind-words to shoo away night,
Filling the sky with a wall of grey light,
Monolith promise of upcoming dawn;

Twinkles of glimmerings wink through its grey;
Light-diamonds, lust-diamonds, herald thy Day.

MOTHER'S DAY, MAY 11, 2003

The paper that I used to pen these lines
Was used, upon the other side, for math.
I am no crank who claims a direct path
Leads from the letters to the number-signs;

The letters spell my feelings, and impart,
For amatory reasons, what I think
Via a structured artwork, framed in ink,
But sculptured from my architectured heart;

The numbers, though, are just my daylight toil;
They only end when thought itself dare end;
And thought itself can easily extend
To bottling up romance, letting it spoil;

And so I write *these* words to compensate
For all the numbers I have penned of late.

BIRTHDAY, JUNE 8, 2003

I am embound within a mesh of numbers
Written by nature, none to be released;
Somewhere is order, somewhere speaks the pattern,
But, like a quilt undone, it can't be pieced;

Unclever are my efforts, fools my nerve cells;
Always what's next is patterned by what's past;
But, just when I think the first will yield the second,
The next-to-last does not reveal the last;

Puzzled I am, smiting my head on air-posts;
I see, in mist, outside my maze, just thee;
But when I hold thee for a moment's respite,
My mental numbers coil and hiss at me.

One day I shall be free of this entrapment;
Till then, I beg of thee, bide near;
When numbers rise to churn my brain asunder,
I think of thee and then I feel quite clear.

WEDDING ANNIVERSARY, JULY 5, 2003

If wanting is wanton, lust unserene,
Then glue is bondage, the moon a handle,
The sky a jug, and a summer night's scene,
Enflamed by a sunset, only a candle.

Thou art entrancing, thy magic a maker
Of sorcerous seraphs. Angels embrace,
Their wingtips embrace alike the waker
And the awoken. Sinuous grace

Smiles as she moves in a mode sentimental
To tether her trust to honesty's pedigree.
I do not degrade what is flat, elemental;
I crown it instead with a textured filigree

Measured by me and enhanced by me,
But openly sculpted and sceptred by thee.

CHRISTMAS, 2003

Some outer joy that does not have a name
Lifts me to write that you have given birth
To a sort of quiet crescendo on my earth,
A consolation prize for loss of fame;

Aging, I strike with footsteps growing slow
Across our lawn, half-frozen half the year,
Half-damp with dew when April-May is near,
Half halt with dryness in September's glow.

Surely this sudden calm cannot be right.
Should not my urgings flail once more the mist,
Sashay across dark moorings to some tryst,
Block off with blinders all ambitions' sight?

No, for my calm has told me, donoress,
That nameless joy is simply happiness.

NEW YEAR, JANUARY 1, 2004

Thus to creating fell my lonely mind
That sought reasons to give for what occurred
Should love make flagellation of the blind
A possible, and deafness to be heard;

There are no moral systems hold me fast
Or ideologies pulling me by the boot;
Only a one abstraction seems to last,
The law that says desire is at the root

Of all we do and think and bring to pass;
Where am I if my one and only thought
Is something just conceptual, sounding brass,
And not desire that I have always sought?

These words are symbols of desire (for me),
And they spring full-fathomed from my pen (for thee).

ST. VALENTINE'S DAY, 2004

In this aggrieved climate Thou art warmth:
Thou fosterest grass to grow beneath the snows;
Thine elegant smile encourages re-birth
Of leaflings on the clematis that grows

Up and along its fences of grey pine;
Thine eyes, tinctured with dusk and browny gold,
Laser with light the flowers that intertwine,
Glossy in summer, grimmer in the cold,

But ready to grow in warmness borne from Night;
Lightness Thou art, with Dark from Courage forged;
Sunblaze Thou art when Sun has gone from sight;
Pleasure Thou art and Nature herself is gorged

With Thy gifts and all Thy tendered offerings;
Thou *art*; and so my Art can see these things.

MOTHER'S DAY, MAY 9, 2004

When I am ill, you work your magic ways
To chasten Nature, forcing it to hide
Behind its beauty to plot for later days
When death and fear might battle side by side;

Bur thou art mental Beauty, thou wilt stand
Strong against the onslaught of that force
That causes mindless Nature to expand
And drag our human natures from their course;

Thou art fierce force that never loses fight:
Nature thou mouldest into healthy grace;
Already my petty battlings seem trite;
Already my verse seems somewhat out of place;

For how could I live without your arrant truth?
How could I breathe without you in my bed?
How did I shrug, from times of ancient youth,
Temptations off to which my travels led?

This is for thee my golden epigraph:
Thou stood so firm that when, like a bended tree,
Out of thy clasp I bent, no one dared laugh
Because, like a birch, I always bent back to thee.

SIXTIETH BIRTHDAY, JUNE 8, 2004

I walked around thee, noting
How the world sprang forth in spring:
The flowers that gushed at thy feet
Were yellow-tipped cloudlets floating
Over a haze of grass complete
With counterpoints of emerald emerging;

No camera can capture
What spring with its furbelows did;
Around thee were whitenesses white
Gloating, alongside thy rapture,
And rednesses, bluenesses glowing light,
And purpled phlox and violets a-coveted;

Yet in thy soul do gardens also grow
That flourish through the winter and the snow.

WEDDING ANNIVERSARY, JULY 5, 2004

Against the hills of yesteryear
I saw the sun set into fear;
It pushed its golden rays about
But darkened clouds grew close and near;

Behind black hills the sun's red glow
Lowered itself, deadly, slow;
Night, as it drew its darkness down,
Said I had nowhere I could go;

And just one star lit the Western black
And bit the tunic that was the night;
As sunset left, the star shone more;
The star grew to pinpoint of radiant light;

Poetry's dark is nullified
By noisy pointings, to the moon
And slow-risen stars, as looking down
On loves that ended far too soon;

But poetry's light is sanctified
With inward strength throughout its glow:
You I portray as ethereal;
I as a stargazer, reverent, slow.

CHRISTMAS, 2004

You are the one no harm must come upon.
Upon your shoulders time does bear its weight
And round your outer self outstretches space
Wishing each niche within itself were one
With you; its angularities abate
In *your* space, where its paths run straight
To where, in a distant other space, await
The founders of your strong and headfree race,
The great extension of your marathon
From mother and wife to queen of household grace;
As husband, I keep looking on and on
At a you with whom I scarcely can keep pace,
So rich are the blessings of the aggregate
Of you and your mind and your heart, my paragon.

ST. VALENTINE'S DAY, 2005

I'm writing this in order to declare
That, though you age, I still assert you fair;
Your body has a flesh that pedigree
Of birth from ancient stock can guarantee
Free of fine faults or feinted reddening;
You have a skin whose softness drives me wild
Like escapadings to a wayward child;

And when you are there, standing against the door,
Framed in backlight, silhouetted more
Like a photograph than like a bodied soul,
More like the part of light that makes it whole,
I find your whole complexity maddening!
No painters can encapsulate your looks;
But poets can, in never-ending books.

EASTER, 2005

My way to you is not through silken rhyme
Or arbitrated verse; it is through you,
Whose integrated attitude to time
Makes me a hostage of your tempo too;

You know that time gives nothing that is free
Or adds quiescence to a rambling soul,
But simply ships, across its crescent sea,
Matter to fill whatever was not whole;

And time gives *me* time to look at you afresh
As if our lives had passed in a blink,
Decades had vanished in a single flash,
And you had redesigned my mind to think

More of the days and the sunlight on the grass,
More of the nights with you in coiled sleep,
More of the now; let cloudinesses pass,
And more of you, to hold to and to keep.

MOTHER'S DAY, MAY 8, 2005

In thee I find no mimicking of life;
Life is inside you, thoroughly, through and through;
You make of life a kind of metaphor
Of what it is that changeth "thee" to "you";

Yet still I uphold, in verses such as these,
An arrogant hope, past poetries to praise
And imitate, by preening, their panache
As if no darknesses ever touched our days,

And all that is, forever honeyed is,
As if some dewy god had filled our dawn
With baskets of old errantries gone right
And knights and ladies strolled upon our lawn;

But in our truth, pure life is rarely clean,
And life like thine is very rarely seen.

BIRTHDAY, JUNE 8, 2005

A poem is supposed to be
Less perfect than a lovely tree ...
But what a tree has is its looks;
Poems are monuments in books.

And if this poem ever find
A printer (having sound in mind)
Who stamped its words on pages white,
Then could that printer proudly write

That he had cast those words in gold
To ricochet down years untold
In this, a monument to thee,
Who lovelier art than any tree.

WEDDING ANNIVERSARY, JULY 5, 2005

I am new-bolded, poetry to write
That sings of you exultant; I,
With my pen, pretend you are the sky
That dims old stars that permeated night.

You are my holdfast: you array
The night with newly fixed stars;
You push each one in place; old scars
They are, from wounds from far away.

You are my handhold; you can take
A touching tale of sound and light
And soothe me with it through the night
Till jocund day, like Romeo's, doth break;

You are a helpmate I can hold;
You keep the warmth; you ban the cold.

CHRISTMAS, 2005

It's windy, with a lovely dawn,
And ripples of redness in the sky;
It seems an eloquence speaks down
To spill a speech across the town
That rain will fall, and no birds fly,

And branches break in the waving wind—
So speaks the redness in the sky;
But, while you watch the rain descend,
Think of the light when it all shall end,
Think of the clouds that have all rolled by.

ST. VALENTINE'S DAY, 2006

I send this to where the quiet rivers run,
From thought to thought, within your inner mind;
If you have sought, in friendships, humankind,
Then you will find, in music, union:

Let it enclose you in its quiet arms,
Let its inviolate laws of art stay strong,
Let its enchantments carry you along
And let its spells embrace you with their charms.

For music is mastered time restored again:
Its solemnizing virtues have no end;
It moves relentlessly, like a friend
Whose steadfast help no partner dare disdain;

It enters me when I stand near to you;
And every song I sing of you seems new.

MOTHER'S DAY, MAY 14, 2006

Mountains break and golden hills turn brown
And airy phantoms fill the sunset sky,
When the world looks and sees that you and I
Seem, to each other, to be scarcely known;

For though you never serenaded Earth,
And though I never quilted warmth from care,
Nevertheless our unity is there
As we await our daughter's giving birth;

From two small cells, there will emerge a child
Whose figure will our lotus-days transform,
Much as a figurehead that braves the storm
Can lull to lingering an ocean wild;

Another baby grasps at life's great tree,
Another day will dawn for you and me.

BIRTHDAY, JUNE 8, 2006

An Eastern dawn lights up the star-specked sky
And soon erases every star but one;
It is named Venus and can never die;
It gives a parting glitter to the sun;

But you, for me, are glowing and alive;
Sad dust you are not, no planetary orb,
But bringer, to me, of what makes heavens thrive,
And singer, to me, of songs I can absorb;

As you gaze up into the dawnlight's gold,
Seeing how Venus struggles to stay bright,
Think of yourself as having such a hold
On me that you remain a constant light,

Shattering my darknesses and woes
With words no other person thinks or knows.

WEDDING ANNIVERSARY, JULY 5, 2006

A hundred flowers had watered been by me
When, on my way to fill the watering can,
I trod on a flower that I had failed to see
Faint-opened, in the lawn, to the morning sun;

And, when I think what you have been to me,
I feel so humbled when I find I can
Still speak of what I did not fail to see
When we first met, there in a morning sun

Of Montreal, when your beauty lit in me
A kind of hope that only rarely can
Be kindled in people who have failed to see
How beauty looks its best when morning sun

Shines and illuminates the world we see
Because they never saw, upon a lawn,
Flowers that were too faint to opened be,
And so saw only cloud instead of sun;

The hope you lit in me has lingered on
Through the long canticles of what-should-be
And how or why whatever should-be-done;
But what-you-are, I never fail to see.

CHRISTMAS, 2006

No kind of time stands still when you begin
To move and, halting, place your hand or arm
Upon another's arm; your will to win,
For us and you, a future free from harm
Re-pushes you to new determination;
You know that time moves on, takes no vacation;

And so you move, one leg before the other goes;
You move to catch the wastefulness of those hours
When time left you behind, behind its snows
Of sundry, tawdry days bereft of flowers;
You move till time itself dares let you go
And watches your unflinching progress grow,

As will we all who want you whole again,
Filling our lives with all your soul again.

NEW YEARS EVE, DECEMBER 31, 2006

The highest bells atop the highest towers
Ring out the aged year, a tiring king
Who wielded heft and high majestic powers
But did not change a single vital thing;

The bells ring out into its emptied sky;
The stars do not reverberate, but keep
A visual vigil on eternity
Silently, not knowing how to sleep;

The dying year was one of hurt and shame;
Its autumn leaves were temperate from gloom;
It fizzles out, a water-wetted flame,
But leaves alive our illness-harried home;

And, as the New Year offers up First Day,
I see *its* springtime spread its powers and surge,
Poised upon wingtips merrily in May,
Waiting for sun and you to reemerge.

ST. VALENTINE'S DAY, 2007

A sudden reciprocity can pose
Problems for poets who weave,
Into their words, long passages of prose
That only serve to leave

Tangles of knotlike underwanted thread
That pull their verse
Away from overblownness, yet instead
Drag it to dust or worse;

Your fight deserves far more than normal lines
To rhapsodize its flow;
Diamonds should glitter and fierce designs
With emeralds should glow;

And I would choose, for my gemstone rhyme,
An alexandrite scheme
To fix to the stars of unending time
Poems that would seem

Strong as the strength with which you chose to fight;
But now I quietly see
That silence serves, better than verse, to reignite
A reciprocity.

EASTER, APRIL 5, 2007

It's April and the snow's still coming down,
Wispy betrayals of a spring that's here
Because the buds are budding and full blown
Are the robins' sprints from near to far to near;

But, slowly falling, still the snowflakes fall,
Furnishing reminders of a year
When summer stooped, unable to stand tall,
And bended autumn chilled us all with fear

That you down to the ground would sink too long,
Unable back to your life to penetrate;
But, thanks be to science, we were wrong
And you are once again regenerate,

Living again the way you lived before,
But stronger in strength and wiser from your war.

MOTHER'S DAY, MAY 13, 2007

Music, when it flows from me to you,
May go around you, over, or behind,
But always has a one-intentioned path,
To please you in some manner undesigned;

Always, should loudness be a salient part
Of it, the force and essence of its state
Is the intensity of how I feel;
Anger is absent from its aggregate

And, should an ultra-quietness fall to ground,
This is no silent brooding of my heart,
But represents a quiet, relying strength
On a gossamer bond I cannot pull apart;

And, when in martial movements, thunderclouds
Seem to arise and stack up higher, higher,
Know that their darkness is mere colour-frost
Dampening down the ardour you inspire.

BIRTHDAY, JUNE 8, 2007

This year, a shade of death has shaken me
With a distant whisper of nonconsciousness
And a trembling in my ear of vocal sound—
And you were she who kept me on firm ground;

My lively brain had quite forsaken me.
Caught in a broil of biochemical stress,
It shut me into nothingness, a room,
As it were, of floorlike doorlit gloom;

And you, with the doctor's help, had taken me
From the evil oval of that bio-mess
And brought, assisted, pushed me to a light
That now surrounded you, ousting the night

With whose dark oneness I had been allied:
"In sickness or in health," we're side by side.

THIRTY-FIFTH WEDDING ANNIVERSARY, JULY 5, 2007

If, when I think, I am not writing
Poems to you or if, when singing
To myself a tune, I am inciting
Rebellion in those bardic cells
That potter about my brain, this tells
Me, and warns me, I am bringing

Threat to our anniversary;
I think you find my intellect
A cool and draining adversary
That, running amok in depth, foretells
How waters running deep are wells
That undermine what you respect

About me; their geology
Can cause, like a crack, a sudden fission
Between the Earth, a symbiology
Of fusion-us, and Thought, that quells
Desire and, in its doing so, compels
Foreboding, as if an imposition

Of Thought could fall upon your head,
Thought that could spreaden unconfined,
Or rains of Thought you do not need,
Thought that brings anger that impels
You to shout how Thought expels
Romance; you are furious at my mind;

And so I write two final lines of worry:
I do not want this either, and am sorry.

CHRISTMAS, 2007

Once of a time, you were a gentle girl,
Whose wild simplicity to me was anodyne
And balm unto my all-too-troubled mind;
Others were harsh, but you were keen and kind.

And still, after long years have tugged our worlds
Sometimes to songs we both were urged to sing,
Sometimes to lamentations of regret,
Your kindnesses allow us to forget;

And when insistent work ate up my time,
And illnesses attacked your tender frame,
Your constancy kept, upheld within your hands,
Luminance such as a goddess understands;

And now, as a calm deep snow fills out the night,
Nothing seems wrong and everything seems right.

ST. VALENTINE'S DAY, 2008

I see that secret strength of all you are
And watch, while the spidery snow extinguishes
Each footprint of each passer-by beneath
A layered over-white, how long and far

You walk, facing the frost and the sunrise east
And the morning's spilling of fresh new snow,
Putting each foot strongly ahead, until
You've walked for half a sunny hour at least,

Planting your boots alternately onto the white
While fresh new snow silently falls to hide
The tracks you make as you forward move, ready
To make, and lose, your footprints till the light

Goes darker as the sun spins further west,
Silently sinking your feet to the silent ground,
Silently testing your strength as you make your way,
Silently sensing a new strength manifest.

EASTER, MARCH 23, 2008

We cannot know what weft or warp is woven
Into our tapestried lives by you or me;
Only a god, imagined and unproven,

Or goddess, with quiet duty on her mind,
Would deign to fashion such a majesty
Of fabricated fabric left unsigned;

It's easier to specify our lives as having been
Times we picked out from spaces rarely free
From some run-in with folly unforeseen,

Or daydream born from adolescent woes,
Or deludedness from us, or from *d'autrui*;
Where days that whistled by went, no one knows ...

But nights went to Heaven whenever gratitude
Silenced my breathings to your beatitude.

MOTHER'S DAY, MAY 11, 2008

The morning's light unveils itself at five:
Colourless flowers unfold to show their red;
Magnolias burst to a sprinkled purple-white;
Daylight compellingly spurns the gloom of night;
Surprised, every morning, that still I feel alive,
I leave my warm and well-encumbered bed

To look at the brightening windows' luring in
The growing noise of traffic and of radios on,
And of birds with their intermittencies of song,
And of rustling leaves when the breezes blow more strong,
And of voices unhearable over the matinal din—
These sounds are like echoes from earlier mornings long gone.

And then, while the light commences to prowl each room,
I hear, from the bedroom, motions and stirrings again:
My wife is awaking and stretching and starting to move;
I greedily hope that she's tempted, 'twixt yawnings, to prove
To herself that I, who had once been her clamouring groom,
Am as amorous now and as keen as I had been back then.

BIRTHDAY, JUNE 8, 2008

A single red upon a thronging bush
Of leafy green shows me a glowing rose
That soon will have its counterparts, a spread
Of glowing roses, nature's fingerprints,
That dot the muffled green, in the dusky dawn,
With glowing reds that jolt-incarnadine
A bush that humans bred from nature's seeds.

You are like that for me, a single rose
That springs from a single flower-burst in the spring,
Signaling potentiality;
You temper nature's storm-lights with your glow
And spur me to write new novelties for you,
Verses that fuse her wildness with my words,
And reconcile what's felt with what is true.

WEDDING ANNIVERSARY, JULY 5, 2008

When I see you, small and fragile,
Standing tall beside your chair,
Wishing your heart could be more agile,
Wishing your illnesses were not there,

Then I feel clutched inside,
As if a dreamer had upped and died,
Or as if, in quiet disbelief,
A tree had shriveled to a leaf;

Or as if momentous waterfalls
Were poised to drown our household walls;
Or as if, in a dark inquietude,
Menace engendered ingratitude;

But, when I see your lovely face,
I know you as my saving grace—
You gave me hope to battle on,
You saved me from oblivion—

And so I see you, small and fragile,
Finding a sunlight in all the air,
Spurring your brain to be more agile,
Upbraiding fate for being unfair.

THANKSGIVING, 2008

I have written about you in acres of cumulate verse,
And still the words flow freely; the sight of you
Lit in the doorway, in silhouetted view,
Leads to effusions (and, sometimes, sonnets terse)

Over-idealized, prolix, or worse,
But nobody cares; the words flow warm and free
Like a sepia river that empties into a sea
Whose surfaces its muddy browns immerse;

Or the words clatter, spill on out, diverse.
Nothing you do need stop them, or aught that you say;
On they shall jollily frolic, as if on the way
To a destiny, in a lyrical universe

Of perpetual epitaph, starring the night
With your glory and the fires of my delight.

CHRISTMAS, 2008

Why, when sheer darkness and stifled sorts of shame
Strike your sweet self into sobbing and tears, and you
Know there's no reason for you yourself to blame,
Are you tempted, nevertheless, to self-blame, and you do?

It is because you know that your reasons are great
For fixing faults, as if onto persons, on powers
Whimsical, chance-like, and random that both of us hate
Because they have poisoned and perfidized too many hours

That you could have spent reading books, or knitting,
Or shopping, or watching the news, or on food, but instead
Were emburdened for you with summonses unremitting
To purge the appalling relics that your illness bred;

But, though those hours weighed down on me as well,
I knew your sweet self, inside, would win and would excel.

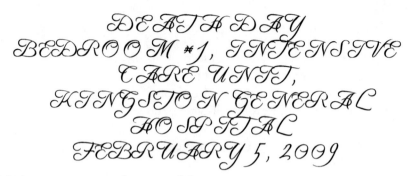

DEATH DAY
BEDROOM #1, INTENSIVE CARE UNIT, KINGSTON GENERAL HOSPITAL
FEBRUARY 5, 2009

Machines no more prolong your life in vain;
Now you lie sleeping like the lovely girl
I first saw sleeping when, in Montreal,
You joined me and my life began again;

Two outward bursts of breath are what betray
To the nurse the final ebbing of your life,
And we are cut off from you, as if a knife
Has tactfully fallen to spirit you away;

But life did not stop; you stayed, your hair and head
A faltering fall of dark against the sheets;
You did not move; the nurse checked whether the beats
Of your pulse had changed to silences instead;

And we stayed on a moment in that place;
And this is that moment's monument to your grace.

FUNERAL DAY
JAMES REID MEMORIAL CHAPEL
KINGSTON, ONTARIO
FEBRUARY 10, 2009

A speech of mine would cut the air with words,
Molest the plangent walls of this quiet house
With fricatives to spin new nothings out
Of threadbare sounds, speak instead of feel;
And all I can feel is her sweet innerness,
Her passionate hatred of badness, and her love
Of literal talk unglossed by metaphors:
Her cooking was supreme and never faddish.
Her mothering was utter and devoted.
Her needlecraft was edifice of patience.
And, every time the night fell on our household,
The next day dawned before the sun had set.
Esther, you were my upwards-leading star;
Your flamelight is impossible to extinguish.

INTERMENT DAY
CATARAQUI CEMETERY, KINGSTON
FEBRUARY 12, 2009

Now are the obsequies over;
The trees near the grave wave arms
Like terriers of winter chasing
Frightening foretastes of spring;
Rain is in the air
And causes gentle meltings
Of the snow on the headstones;
No feelings did you have
As the yellow roses were dropped
Into the ground beside you;
You felt nothing from a puddle
That hollowed the smoothness
Of the earthen sides that hid
The hardness of your urn;
Non-feeling laid its solemn peace
On your ashes, and, out of that peace,
Rose into life this sombre final line:
How *dare* I write that *any one* is "mine"?

HEADSTONE DEDICATION DAY, JUNE 6, 2009

(This poem was read aloud on the occasion of Esther's family's visit from Montreal to view her resting place.)

She is not here to see the gentle grain
Grow in the rains and dews and sunny light
That paper over this golden land again;

She is not here to see the daffodils
Grow high through their leaves of jade and green,
Scenting the earthen odours air distils;

She is not here to see the lilacs out
With their pencils of purple lace and livid white
Jutting and tracing their branches all about;

She is not here to see the April rains
Stumble, from half in snow, to half in sun
Before the cloudings part, and blue regains

Ascendancy across the springtime sky;
She is not here; but will always be nearby.

LaVergne, TN USA
12 January 2010
169637LV00002B/6/P